Hi there

Walk inside, step a little closer, reach deeper
into your consciousness, open the
gates of truth. What will you find?

You'll find meaningful moments,
a place where your intentions are clear,
because there is no better place then
going back to your roots,
deep down, into your heart space of truth.
It's safe and secure, you'll find love
and more things, for sure.

You need to deal with the truth my dear,
to open up the real you, my dear,
to be honest and clear, through mind and heart
in this whole spiritual atmosphere.

"When you begin to see things through
your soul, the mind knows when to shut up,
while the heart feels when to go on."

And so we start at Nightfall, where thoughts fall deep
and memories run high, let's read some stories about
the way of life.

Walk inside, step a little closer and enjoy reading
'balance between the mind & the heart.'

Anastasia

The story
about the owl

I found this little owl,
lying on the ground,
among branches and leaves,
so fragile and cold.

I wrapped this baby owl around my scarf
and gave it some comfort in my room.
With slimy worms and raw meat, this baby owl grew up
and flew back home, at nightfall.

I started writing and I never stopped. It became my
spirit animal and I created my first poetry book with
many meaningful and wise words.

I do not write
to be seen,
I write to be
heard from a
sound people
don't talk about

Words by Anastasia

...a sound deeper
than just words
flying into the air,
meaningless talks,
crazy 'ego' words
coming out of
people's mouth,
like their brains
doesn't match
their soul.

I do not write
to be seen,
I write to be heard
from a sound,
a sound of people's
imperfections,
a sound of people's
vulnerability,
a sound that lasts forever,
'cause words fade away,
eyes can get lost, but
the soul stays present.

The purpose of life my dear, is to feel...

...'cause if there's nothing to feel,
then why is your soul
reaching through your core,
healing all of your hidden flaws?

If there's nothing to feel,
then why is your heart
grounded into your body,
wrapped around every cell
in search for love?

If there's nothing to feel,
then why is your spirit guide
streaming through your veins,
feeding you some logic
for your brains?

...and if there's so
much to feel,
but you keep running
somewhere left behind
while the answers
to your restless mind,
lies into your
very own heart.

if you can't feel
what's going on
inside your heart

then how can
you manage a
life you want?

Words by Anastasia

...if you can't feel
what you need,
then how can you
go in search
for something new?
You want it all clear,
but you can't dissapear
out of fear,
your heart is pulling
you back to what
you can call...love,
my dear.

"What comes from
your soul will flow
through your heart
and what flows
through your heart
will be seen by the world."

Manage the life
you want
by going back inside
your heart,
where it all feels
like home.

at some point in
your life you'll
get a wake-up call

to let go of all
the logic and to
fall down into the
bottom of your heart

Words by Anastasia

...to fall down hard
so make sure the
bottom of your heart
feels soft and secure.
At some point,
some things and
some people,
some situations
and some places
are meant to be,
'cause that's how
you'll get to see
the beauty of
your inner being.

Logic will keep
you aware of
what's best for you
at this time & moment,
but the heart
will keep you aware
of what's best,
all your life...
Fall down into the
bottom of your heart
where it all feels right.

Born & raised...

Born and raised with your mind,
but if you want a new start,
then grow and change
from your heart.

Born and raised to reach
your dreams and goals,
but if you want a new start,
then grow and change
in the present moment.

Born and raised with a consistency
of your thoughts,
but if you want a new start,
then grow and change
out of love.

in the process of change,
you go deep
into the unknown,
by feeling
something all along

Words by Anastasia

14

...you go deep
into the unknown,
doing things
unpleasant, feeling
things different,
stepping into
a period of
not knowing how
it will be in a
few months, but
each day is one
step closer to
changes that will
bring you to
something better & bigger,
something more you
and less someone else,
something real & authentic,
deeper & more intriguer,
'cause in the process
of change, how did you
expect to grow if you keep
running in circles,
while deep down
you're feeling
something... all along?

The Unknown

Let's fly into
the unknown
for a change,

strong and brave
facing some fears
to all what's
going on,

taking a few
steps back,
to realize there's
more to get,

let's fly into
the unknown
for a change,

to embrace love,
to dive deep
into what feels
like home,
to be yourself
and nothing more.

Alone time

Alone time is needed
to reset your soul
while everybody
is gone, 'cause
your can't reset
your life by
replaying the old,

to hear your own voice
far away from people
who are a distraction
for your own choice.

It's a shame, these days,
people can't be alone,
afraid of being
on there own?

If there's something
you should know,
being alone is the
most precious thing
to grow,
one step closer
to what's meant
to be yours.

you don't have to
force anything
if your intentions
are real, if, what
you do, has meaning

Words by Anastasia

...the wrong things
happen if you force
anything that is not
giving you freely,
if you force to believe
what you can't see.

You can't force
anything, and if
you do...it will break
the passion you
once had, in this
exhausted feeling
you now have.

going there
won't hurt,
if what
you do is
out of love

Words by Anastasia

...going there,
whatever 'there'
means for you,
something new,
a change, a closure,
healing, walking away,
it won't hurt, if what
you do has meaning.
Doing things
out of ego won't last
and mostly, one day,
it hurts.

"You're always
gaining strength,
by doing the right thing."

A heart filled with
true experiences
and real stories
are better than
an ego surrounded
with regrets and guilt,
the opposite of
being down to earth.

Who you are now...

...who you are now,
is only because you
give yourself the
chance to grow
by taking risks,
by falling, by getting
into the unknown,

'cause that's the only
way to get your soul
to where it belongs,
to feel the real
pleasure of joy.

"Do not stay small
when the soul
wants to grow."

Who you are now,
is only because you
give yourself the
chance to rise above,
to fall in love,
to move along
and to stay strong.

the first step
to heal is
loneliness,

to find that
deeper level
through all
the emptiness,

'cause you can
handle anything
after handeling
your own darkness

Words by Anastasia

...a darkness everyone
wants to avoid,
but needs to embrace,
exposed with yourself
and no one else.
No reason to run
from your own
healing process
because your soul
is in need for change.

"All the things
that hurt are
not yet healed,
the words
you speak
must be felt,
in order to take
action of
what you feel."

That, my dear,
is the purpose
of life, to be real.

you don't need
to forget
the past, my love

it has shaped you
until this day

but you need
to step away

from a story
that doesn't
serve you anymore

Words by Anastasia

...a story that
doesn't serve
you anymore
because it has shaped
you into the person
you are today,
but there is a future
that doesn't have
to be this way...

don't forget,
don't regret,
it all has its purpose,
to shape you into
the person you
are meant to be.

"Everyone has a
story to tell, if not now,
someday, something,
is preparing you
for the next step.
If not now, someday,
somehow, you'll need
to stay true to yourself."

you keep walking
back and forth
into your own heart,
stuck, unable to get out

you keep yourself blocked,
chains wrapped around
your inner compass,
unable to unlock

but you need to
open up that inner part
of your stainless
stubborn heart

to let the past... get out

Words by Anastasia

28

...a traumatic heart
can't open up for love,
'cause it hurts, it keeps the pain
alive, stays in the past,
unable to let go of a story
that once was, but now gone.

It feels safe, but homeless,
it feels colorful, but dark,
it feels real, but fake,
'cause you're not here
but there...in the dark.

A stubborn heart will not
lead you to a new start,
the past can't make
new moments,
only dark memories,
so dark, you can't find the
light of you inner compass.

If you lost track by mind,
follow the road by heart.
If you lost track by sight,
follow the eyes of love.

Strong people

Some strong people
by your side build up
a strong foundation
for life,
family and history,
friends and a little
bit of mystery,

never underestimate
each moment to celebrate,
with people and all the
little things to appreciate.

To tell stories with flair,
to laugh from the
inside out, to have fun,
to drink a little more,
to think a little less,

and to appreciate
the people who
share the same love.

Total change

We all think
we've made it
at a certain age,
but don't be so
sure about that,
'cause that certain
age, one day,
can bring you
a total change.

If it's yours to keep,
it will reach deep
with ups and downs,
highs and lows
but never out of reach.

If it's yours to keep,
it will stay on the
surface and never
out of reach.

Life it not meant
to stay in course,
but surprises you
with many experiences
of growth & love.

stories from the heart
are more worth feeling,
than memories of the mind,
who keep you restless in the past

...restless in the past,
memories that flee,
thoughts that once
had a story but
changed from direction
you can't reach
anymore,
you can't change
anymore,

restless in the past,
memories that
brought life, to a time,
based somewhere
in your mind but lost
the meaning of your heart,

but a story worth feeling
is meant to last,
a story from the heart
keeps you grounded
for life.

"When you begin
to see things through
your soul, the mind
knows when to shut up,
while the heart feels
when to go on."

if you don't
make it count,
then life
surprises
you with never
ending stories
of doubt

Words by Anastasia

...these never ending stories
leads to no real one.
Never ending stories
keeps you going
in circles of insecurities,
no closure,
spinning around
with the same old stories,
people and situations.

This energy speaks
for itself, no real devotion
with no real emotions, right?
There is no doubt,
if what comes from
the heart is true and
worth exploring.

You'll make something
or someone count
if it's true and authentic,
because it matches the
frequency of your inner self.

If you don't make it count,
life will surprises you
with never ending stories
all...because of yourself.

& it's practical and
logical, but does
it match the
frequency of your
heart's desire?

Words by Anastasia

...too much logic
causes situations
of confusion,
situations of 'what if'
of 'what should I do'
kinda thoughts,
they slow down
things that truly
belong to you.

Feel in the right
direction, 'cause
the wrong one
will bring you
to fake places
and meaningless
situations.

"Logic can't speak
in feelings and
thoughts can't
think in moments."

Everyday, all day
we have these
moments to live,
to act and to feel.
The right decisions
and actions start
from within,
the heart.

you can't expect
the answers to
your questions
if, you keep
surrounding yourself
with people who
aren't the answer
to begin with

Words by Anastasia

...in need for the right answers
you need to start asking the
right questions, to and for yourself.

In order to grow from a painful
experience, in order to learn
from the past, you need to be
honest, to and for yourself.

It will give you the answers you,
deep inside, already feel.

When the heart feels warm...

...when the heart
feels warm,
safe in space,
grounded on earth,
it doesn't feel pain,
it doesn't go back
in the past, where
it all feels cold.

When the heart
feels warm, it
circulates a stream
into the human soul,
it goes up and down,
in and out, ready for
love and to open up,
not going back,
'cause there is no
reason to stand
in the cold.

When the heart
feels warm, it
ciculates the
movement into
little steps
of...progress.

Heaven on earth

Heaven on earth,
for those understanding
the deeper meaning
of your own worth.

Heaven on earth,
for those understanding
that the 'little things'
are the big ones.

Be in balance with
body & mind,
soul & heart,
to eventually
feel true love
in all his form.

True love for yourself
and true love in a
significant other,
or any kind of
situation grounded
out of love.

Heaven on earth,
for those understanding
that knowlegde comes
from the mind and
wisdom grows
from the heart.

There is so much
heaven on earth,
but first, you must
appreciate your
own worth.

a story felt
by the heart,
is mostly loved,
real and true
from the start

Words by Anastasia

...a story felt
by the heart,
not necessary
to think very hard,
it goes naturally,
it feels good,
you'll see, you can
trust all what comes
from a place where
it feels safe.

Stories from
the heart are
more worth
feeling, than
memories from
the mind, who
keep you restless
in the past, but
a story worth feeling
is meant to last.

"A natural ability
has no thoughts,
it flows intuitive,
together with a
powerful tranquility."

it needs to
be a choice,

yours

Words by Anastasia

...you have a voice
of your own, you know,
ready to make choices
far away of other voices,
streaming into
the veins of your ears.

Let them talk
their way, take your
time to believe
what is truly yours,
a choice made
by your inner voice,
not by people
that doesn't know
what is yours,
how you feel and
which things
you want...

It needs to be
a choice you know,
it represents
authenticity,
an identity that
doesn't feel lost,

don't forget
to be happy
with yourself,
rather for
someone else

Words by Anastasia

...you will be stronger
for it in the long run,
finding inner peace
just for yourself,
knowing what
you want, like love,
being complete
with yourself,
here on earth.

Ground yourself
to know what
true love is,
to feel the need
to share,
ready to care,
for yourself
and others.

Conditioned out
of love

Conditioned out of love,
brings different answers
to what's meant, to be yours.

Conditioned out of love,
is a true feeling that
starts from within, to grow.

Conditioned out of love,
will always plant a seed
with the right answers
and true feelings, in need.

The moment you
realize your mindset
out of ego doesn't bring
you anywhere, but far,
far away from the heart.

Whatever is
on your mind

Whatever is on your mind,
it's been felt by the heart,
a mysterious feeling
that is bothering you
but must be felt
for you to grow.

Whatever is on you mind,
you need time to
experience your
own do's and don'ts.

Standing on the crossroads
of your mind, walking on
the highway of your heart,
choose to learn the
language of yourself,
'cause it's only meant
for you to show what's
like to be your true self.

You can't have it all...

...you can't have
it all, but you can
watch something grow.

You can't have it all,
but what you have now
is already much more,
than a few months ago.

You can't have it all,
but who you are now
has grown more,
than a few weeks ago.

Patience, is what
you need to grow,
go with the flow,
it doesn't need
to hurry and so on...

You can't have it all,
but what you do now
is already better,
than a few days ago.

you know,
because
you feel

...you know something,
because you feel it first.
In a world of morality
it is your heart, your
intuition that speaks
above the mind.
You don't walk through
life just by 'thinking',
you walk through life
by experience the
messages of the heart,
by experience moments
of your soul, by experience
messages you feel and love.

There's too much to
think about, but there's
only one thing to feel,
so feel the mind, by heart.

...and in the end,
everything in life
needs to feel natural

Words by Anastasia

...life will present
you the opposite,
if you're not following
your own path
of...authenticity,
'cause that's where
the beauty lies
of simplicity.

One day life will
feel natural
on a higher level,
if your intuition
speaks on a
deeper level,
if you're following
your true worth
and not through
someone else.

In the end, if it
doesn't feel natural,
goes natural of things
aren't going anywhere,
then one day,
it's going...nowhere.

" ...and suddenly
you will discover that,
the people you meet
and the places you go,
are part of your
soul's plan. „

Words by Anastasia

"She
meets so many people
through eyes and words,
but it's only the
soul she cares for."

Wordd by Anastasia

Lots of love,
Anastasia

Lightning Source UK Ltd.
Milton Keynes UK
UKHW020947191021
392419UK00007B/492

Faithfulness in Our Day to Day Life

Dr. Chandrakumar Manickam

Parson Place Press
Mobile, Alabama

ISBN 10: 0-9786567-1-7
ISBN 13: 978-0-9786567-1-3

Library of Congress Control Number: 2007928932

Endorsements

"In this book, Chandrakumar Manickam passionately and eloquently calls us to be faithful to God. This wealth of solid, Scripture-based counsel and exhortation will help transform your relationship with God. If you want to know how to give account to God for your inner thoughts, motives, words and actions, then you have picked up the right book."

Dr. B. K. Pramanik,
CEO and General Secretary
Bible Society of India

"Thank you for taking time to teach at our Bible school, and to our congregation. Every minute of it was a blessing, and we do look forward to your return. We do appreciate your coming out here to us."

Jens Garnfeldt
Senior Pastor, Kopenhagen Bible Training Center
Denmark

"Thank you for ministering in our midst. Your sharing is an encouragement to our students to become itinerant evangelists."

Rev. Ronald Yu
Director, Chinese Mission Seminary
Hong Kong

Other Books by This Author

TABLE OF CONTENTS

The Author's Note

I thank God for not only motivating me, but also for enabling me to write this book at the most needed hour. We live in an era of compromise. As I travel around this world, I find that very few Christians are faithful in fulfilling their God-given responsibilities. There has been a tremendous response to this message whenever I have preached it in some Pastors and Christian leaders' conferences. Hence, it is my sincere prayer that the contents of this book may inspire and motivate all the believers in Christ not to be compromisers, but overcomers.

Dr. Chandrakumar Manickam

I dedicate this book to my dear wife, **Dr. SARA KASTHURI**, and to my precious daughter, **Dr. RUTH SNEHA**, who have always stood with me in full co-operation in order to live a faithful, uncompromising life together, pleasing to the Lord.

Dr. Chandrakumar Manickam

Foreword

Probably the most important word for faithfulness in Christian living is *commitment*. Commitment to the Christian is primarily to a person, the Lord Jesus Christ. But it has to be a programme also, because the Lord Jesus Christ came to announce the kingdom of God. So, commitment to the Christian is also to the kingdom of God. But then, the kingdom is not in abstract terms, it is in concrete relationships. But commitment to the Christian is to human beings. Such a commitment to the Lord Jesus Christ, the kingdom of God, and to human beings cannot be expressed without the proper use of all the means that are within the Christian's control. And hence, in this very remarkably terse effort, Dr. Chandrakumar has attempted to state faithfulness in Christian living in all these contexts.

There is an element about faithfulness that we dare not overlook. Someone said, "Talent attracts talent." I suppose it is the same as saying, "like begets like." There is nothing like faithfulness in other people around us. Somehow, a person who has maintained his commitment to the Lord and His kingdom and people around him, evokes in those who are in contact with him a similar nature or quality. John Newton, the famous composer of the hymn, "Amazing Grace", was one such person.

In 1785, while he was the distinguished pastor of St. Mary Woolnoth in London, he drew the attention of William Wilberforce, the young, brilliant politician. Wilberforce was only 26, but already a member of the parliament. His friends had predicted a great political career for him. At that time, Wilberforce had recently experienced a religious awakening. The now "reborn" Wilberforce sought out the 64 year old Newton for counsel. He wanted to know if he should resign from parliament and enter the ministry. Newton advised him to remain where he was in politics. "God can make you a blessing, both as a Christian and as a Statesman."

But young Wilberforce was looking for a cause, and Newton preached against slavery. But this was too costly for any political party to dare touch. And it was also a cause that no true Christian could evade.

Newton spoke from personal experience. He had been on the course of Africa as a broken man who had command of a slave ship. It was from this degradation that he had tasted "Amazing Grace." He addressed the Privy Council, which included Prime Minister William Pitt, and said, "The slaves lie in two rows, one above the other, on each side of the ship, like books upon a shelf. The poor creatures are in irons, both hands and feet. And every morning more instances than one are found of the living and the dead fastened together."

In March 1807, the Parliament passed the Wilberforce Bill abolishing slavery. And on December 21, 1807, the Rev. John Newton, then 82 years old, spoke his last words, "I am a great sinner, and Christ is a great Saviour."

Faithfulness in one produces faithfulness in another. And the chain is unending.

May such history-making, history-changing, faithfulness immerge in the heart and life of every reader of this book so that the great contagion of faithfulness would spread across the nations in the hearts and lives of every true believer. And may the Lord grant it so! Hallelujah!

Rev. Dr. Samuel Kamaleson
World Vision International

INTRODUCTION

We live in an era of compromise. Very few are faithful in fulfilling their God-given responsibilities. Through our lives we follow the path of least resistance. We hold on to a conviction only till it gets in the way of our comfort, and we maintain a standard as long as it does not hinder something we wish to do. Sometimes we even go down on the principles we claim to follow to accomplish our selfish goals. Such a self-centered, worldly perspective is so widespread that we essentially live in a world of compromise. Hence, we are going to discuss in this book as to how we can live an uncompromising, faithful Christian life.

What is Faithfulness?

The Greek word for faithfulness is **Pistos**, which means trustworthiness, reliability, confidence, and so on. Faithfulness is an attribute or quality applied in the Bible to both God and Man. When used of God, it has in the Old Testament a two-fold emphasis, referring first to his absolute reliability, firm constancy, and complete freedom from arbitrariness or fickleness, and secondly, to his steadfast, loyal love toward his people and his loyalty. He is faithful in keeping his promises and is therefore worthy of trust. When used of man, the Bible exhorts men to be faithful in fulfilling their God-given responsibilities and to be loyal to him.

Chapter - 1
Faithfulness in Thoughts and Words

First of all God expects us to be faithful in our private life, this is very important and highly essential. If we are not faithful to God in our private life we cannot be faithful to Him in our public life. Our Lord Jesus made it very clear to James and John that the highest positions are reserved for those who have qualified in secret, that is, in their private life. We must be faithful to the Lord in our thoughts, words, motives, actions and in our relationships with each other.

1. Faithful in Thoughts

Regarding the thought life, we find an order established in **Rom. 1:21-32**. We read in **verse 21** "For even though they knew God, they did not honour Him as God or give thanks; but they became futile in their speculations and their foolish heart was darkened."

We see that they knew God, but they became vain in their reasoning. This is concerning their thought life. We read in **verse 22** "Professing to be wise, they became fools." This professing was taking place internally and we see the action externally in **verse 23** "And exchanged the glory of the incorruptible man and of birds and four footed animals and crawling creatures." In **verse 24** we read the result: "Therefore God gave them over in the lusts of their hearts to impurity, that their bodies might be dis-honoured among them." Thus we see the order. First there was an idea in their thought life and then came the external action and then follows the consequences of this action. If we are faithful, truthful, sincere and open to the conviction and correction of the Holy Spirit of God in our internal thought life, then, the external result will be a true spiritual life. Moral or spiritual battles are not won in the external world first. They are always a result flowing naturally from a cause, and the cause is in the internal world of one's thoughts.

Emphasising this fact with a great force, Jesus said, "You brood of vipers, how can you, being evil, speak what is good? For the mouth speaks out of that which fills the heart" **(Matt. 12:34).** "Not what enters into the mouth defiles the man, but what proceeds out of the mouth, this defiles the man" **(Matt. 15:11).** Again it is the internal that Jesus stresses upon. The internal comes before the external and the internal produces the external. It is a matter of cause and effect.

Even in the Sermon on the Mount, Jesus deals with this aspect. Jesus said, "Whosoever is angry with his brother without a cause shall be in danger of the judgement" **(Matt. 5:21,22).**

Compare this with **1 Jn. 3:15,** "Everyone who
hates his brother is a murderer...." Jesus also
said in **Matthew 5:28** that, "...everyone who
looks on a woman with lust for her has already
committed adultery with her in his heart." So,
we can be deadly sinners in our thought life,
which is equally condemned and would be dealt
with severely by our righteous Judge. So, we
are accountable to God for the thoughts that we
think. We need to exercise ourselves to keep
our thoughts pure and clean and should be
inwardly faithful to the Lord.

2. Faithful in Words

We must also be faithful to the Lord in our
word life. Are the words that come out of our
lips true to our conscience? Sometimes the
actual truth is far away from the words that
come out of us. Some times we hide bitterness
in our hearts towards a person and talk to him
with sugar-coated words. The Psalmist says
that a wicked man's words are smoother than
cream, but there is hatred in his heart; his
words are as soothing as oil, but they cut like
sharp swords **(Ps. 55:21)**.

We read in **Prov. 10:18,** "He who conceals
hatred has lying lips..." Do we have lying lips?
"Lying lips are an abomination to the Lord, but
those who deal faithfully are his delight"
(Prov. 12:22). The word faithful here means
our faithfulness in our word life. "Truthful lips

will be established forever, but a lying tongue is only for a moment" **(Prov. 12:19)**. The Word of God warns us severely against lying lips. There is no such thing as a black lie, red lie or white lie. A lie is a lie. "Do not lie to one another, since you laid aside the old self with its evil practices..." **(Col. 3:9).** It is an evil practice. We read in **Revelation 21:8,** "But for the cowardly and unbelieving and abominable and murderers and immoral persons and sorcerers and idolaters and all liars, their part will be in the lake that burns with fire and brimstone, which is the second death." Here we see that liars are equally compared with murderers and immoral persons.

Nothing unclean and no one who practices abomination and lying shall ever enter into heaven **(Rev. 21:27).** Outside heaven would be dogs and the sorcerers and the immoral persons and the murderers and the idolaters and everyone who loves and practices lying **(Rev. 22:15).** We read in **Revelation 14:4,5** about the **144,000** witnesses that, these are the ones who follow the lamb wherever He goes and no lie was found in their mouth; they are blameless. So, let us have the fear of the Lord in our word life, for every word we speak we need to give account to the Lord. Jesus said, "And I say to you that every careless word that men shall speak, they shall render account for it in the day of judgment" **(Matt. 12:36,37).**

"Do not let any unwholesome talk come out of your mouths, but only what is helpful for building others up according to their needs, that it may benefit those who listen" **(Eph. 4:29 NIV).** "Let your speech always be with grace, seasoned, as it were with salt, so that you may know how you should respond to each person" **(Col. 4:6 NIV).**

"Every man has a right to his opinion, but no man has a right to be wrong in his facts." - **Bernard M. B**.

Chapter - 2
Faithfulness in Motives and Actions

In our private life we must be faithful to the Lord in our motives and actions. We do certain things and perform certain actions with certain motives. There is a possibility that we can do right things with wrong motives. Sometimes we can help or support others or be good or talk nicely to them with a wrong motive of some personal security or gain.

Even God makes His motives clear before taking any action. He tells the people of Israel, "I had concern for My holy name. Therefore, it is not for your sake, O house of Israel, that I am going to do these things, but for the sake of My holy name, which you have profaned among the nations where you have gone." **(Ezek. 36:21-23)**.

God saved the people of Israel for His name's sake, to make His mighty power known **(Ps. 106:8)**.

Jesus said, "Be careful not to do your 'acts of righteousness' before men, to be seen by them. If you do, you will have no reward from your Father in heaven. So, when you give to the needy, do not announce it with trumpets, as the hypocrites do in the synagogues and on the streets, to be honored by men. I tell you the truth; they have received their reward in full. But when you give to the needy, do not let your left hand know what your right hand is doing, so that your giving may be in secret. When you pray, do not be like the hypocrites, for they love to pray standing in the synagogues and on the street corners to be seen by men. Then your Father, who sees what is done in secret, will reward you." **(Matt. 6:1-6)**.

So, we have to be extremely careful in this and should always judge our motives and keep them open to the correction and conviction of the Holy Spirit of God.

Chapter - 3
Faithfulness in Money Matters

We must be faithful to God in our Penny life, in our money matters. We have been told since childhood that money talks. **Ray. O. Jones** tells us of what a dollar or a rupee note would speak. It would say, "You hold me in your hand and call me yours. Yet may I not as well call you mine. See, How easily I rule you. To gain me, you hold me in your hand and call me yours. Yet may I not as well call you mine. See, how easily I rule you. To gain me, you would all but die. I am impersonal as rain, essential as water. Without me, men and institutions would die, yet I do not hold the power of life for them; I am futile without the stamp of your desire. I go nowhere unless you send me. I keep strange company. For me, men mock, love and scorn character. Yet I am appointed to the service of saints, to give education to the growing mind and food to the starving bodies of the poor. My power is terrific. Handle me carefully and wisely, lest you become my servant rather than I yours."

John D. Rockfeller said, "The poorest man I know is the man who has nothing but money." Money may be the husk of many things, but not the kernel. It brings you food, but not appetite; medicine, but not health; acquaintances, but not friends; servants, but not loyalty; days of joy, but not peace or happiness - **Henrik Ibsen**. "A man's life is not made secure by what he owns, even when he has more than he needs." **(Lk. 12:15).** Riches are like salt water - the more you drink the more you thirst.

It is good to find out what the mind of Christ is, to think as He thought, and to feel just as He felt in money matters. In this world money is the standard of value. The world loves it, seeks it above everything and often worships it. It is the standard of value not only for material things, but also for man himself, as man is too often valued according to his money. Not only in the kingdom of this world, but in the kingdom of heaven too, a man is judged by his money but on a different principle.

The world asks, what does a man own? Christ asks how does he use it? The world is concerned about getting money but Christ is concerned about giving money. The world asks, what does he give? Christ asks, how does he give? The world looks at the money and its amount, Christ at the man and his motive. We study about it in the story of the poor widow **(Mk. 12:41-44).** Many that were rich cast in much, but it was out of their abundance; there was no real sacrifice in it; their life was easy and comfortable as ever, it cost them nothing. Here we see the poor widow cast in all that she had, even all her living.

When David wanted to buy land to build an altar to the Lord, that land was offered free of cost to him, but he refused and said in **2 Sam. 24:24**, "I will not offer burnt offerings to the Lord my God which cost me nothing."

The world asks how much a man gives. Christ asks how much he keeps. The world looks at the gift. Christ asks whether the gift was a sacrifice. The widow's gift won the heart of Christ and His approval, for it was in the spirit of His own self-sacrifice, who being rich became poor for our sakes. We need to be faithful in our giving. Money given in the spirit of self-sacrifice and love and faith in Him who has paid all, brings a rich, and eternal reward.

When the Holy Spirit of God came down at Pentecost to dwell in men, He assumed charge and control of their whole life. He took charge of their penny life too. He taught giving to the church and sharing with each other. He also tested their inner motives in their giving. We see in **(Acts. 5:1-11)** that Ananias and Saphira sold a possession and kept back part of the price, and Ananias brought the remaining portion and laid it at the feet of the apostles. But both of them were smitten dead by God. Why did this happen? This was because they were not faithful in their giving. It is not the question of whether they gave all that they possessed but whether they gave all that they professed. Here we see a very sad thing. Both the husband and wife plotted this affair and joined hands and lied not against men but against the Holy Spirit of God.

A Russian proverb says, "When money speaks, the truth is silent." We must be truthful in all our money matters and give correct accounts even in our secular job. Robert Frost humorously said,

> *"Never ask of money spent,*
> *Where the spender thinks it went*
> *Nobody was ever meant,*
> *to remember or invent*
> *What he did with every cent."*

So, every faithful Christian should be faithful in his penny life, as he has to give account to God for every penny, which he receives and spends. You can't take your money to heaven, but you can make an investment for eternity. Some people have plenty to live on, but nothing to live for.

Chapter - 4
Faithfulness of Christian Minorities in the Dark Ages

We must be faithful to the Lord even in the midst of persecution. When our Lord Jesus was pleased to take upon Himself the form of a servant and go about preaching the kingdom of God, He took all opportunities to forewarn His disciples of the many distresses, afflictions and persecutions they must expect to endure for His name's sake. The apostle Paul, following the steps of our Lord, takes particular care to warn young Timothy of the difficulties he must expect to meet within the course of his ministry.

Though all face persecutions, yet it may be in differing degrees; and all Christians will find by their own experience that whether they act in a private or public capacity they must in some degree or other suffer persecution. Not all who are persecuted are real Christians, for many sometimes suffer and are persecuted for having done wrong rather than for righteousness sake. The most important question is, are you still faithful to God in spite of being persecuted for godly living?

It is estimated that more than 50 million Christians died for their faith in the dark ages. A million Christians died for their faith when the communists seized China; innumerable thousands died as martyrs in Africa and so on.

1. Why should we expect persecution?

(i) First, because our Lord taught in **Matt. 5.10,** "Blessed are those who are persecuted because of righteousness."

(ii) Secondly, because our Lord Himself experienced it. Follow the Lord from the manger to the cross and check whether we have gone through any persecution, which was like that of the Son of God while He was on the planet earth. He was hated by wicked men, reviled, counted and called a blasphemer, a drunkard, a Samaritan, and a devil; He was stoned, thrust out of the synagogues, called a deceiver of people, and as an enemy of Caesar scourged, spit upon, condemned and nailed to an accursed tree.

(iii) Thirdly, because the saints of all ages experienced it and are experiencing it. We see how Abel was made a martyr for his religion and how the son of the bond-woman mocked Isaac. As we read the Acts of the Apostles, we see how the early Christians were

threatened,   stoned,   imprisoned,
scourged and martyred. Even today
many saints in the communist lands
are undergoing severe persecutions.

(iv) Fourthly, Because of the sinner's
enemity against God. Wicked men hate
God and therefore cannot but hate
those who are Godly.

(v) Fifthly, because the Godly need it. Why
should the Godly go through suffering
and persecution? The Apostle Paul in
his letter to the Corinthians lifts the
veil of his private life and allows us to
catch a glimpse of his human frailties
and needs. He very clearly records the
specifics of his anguish, tears, affliction
and satanic opposition, with details of
his persecution, loneliness, imprison-
ments, beatings, feelings of despair,
hunger, ship-wrecks, sleepless nights
and that "thorn in the flesh" — his
companion of pain. It makes us feel
close to him, as we picture him as a
man with real down to earth problems
just like you and me. For our suffering
and persecution Paul gives three
reasons in **2 Cor. 1:3-11:**

1. "That we may be able to comfort those
who are in any affliction..." **(verse 4).**

God allows suffering so that we might have the capacity to enter into the sorrows and afflictions of others. If you have suffered the loss of your husband or your wife or your child, you would be in complete sympathy with some one else with a similar kind of a loss. We are able to have a better understanding of their situation.

2. "That we should not trust in ourselves..." **(verse 9).** God also allows suffering and persecution in our lives so that we might learn what it means to depend on Him, not on our own strength and resources. Again and again He reminds us of the consequences of pride, but sometimes only through suffering do we learn the lesson.

3. "That thanks may be given..."**(verse 11).** God trains us to give thanks in everything. Sometimes, one of the reasons why our suffering is prolonged is that we take so long to say "Thank you, Lord, for this suffering or this experience."

"How unfinished and rebellious and proud and unconcerned we would be without suffering!" said **Charles Swindoll.**

(b) What have we endured for the Lord?

A man writes about his dream, which is quoted in the Presbyterian survey. It goes as follows: I saw in a dream that I was in the heavenly and celestial city, though when and how I got there I could not tell. I saw one of a great multitude which no man could number, from all countries and peoples and times and ages. Somehow I found that the saint who stood next to me had been in heaven, more than 1,860 years. "Who are you?" I said to him. (We both spoke the same languages of heavenly Canaan, so I understood him and he me). "I" said he, "was a Roman Christian; I lived in the days of the Apostle Paul; I was one of those who died in Nero's persecutions. I was covered with pitch and fastened to a stake and set on fire to light up Nero's gardens."

"How awful," I exclaimed. "No" he said, "I was glad to do something for Jesus. He died on the cross for me." The man on the other side then spoke, "I have been in Heaven only a few hundred years. I came from an island in the Southern seas – Erromanga. John Williams, a missionary, came and told me about Jesus, and

I too learned to love Him. My fellow country-men killed the missionary, and they caught and bound me. I was beaten until I fainted and they thought I was dead, but I revived. The next day they knocked me on the head, cooked and ate me."

"How terrible," I said. "NO" he answered, "I was glad to die as a Christian. You see the missionaries had told me that Jesus was scourged and crowned with thorns for me." Then they both turned to me and asked, "What did you suffer for him? Or did you sell what you have had for the money which sent men like John Williams to tell the heathen about Jesus?" "And I was speechless. And while they both were looking at me with sorrowful eyes, I awoke, and it was a dream. But I lay on my soft bed awake for hours, thinking of the money I had wasted on my own pleasures; or my extra clothing, and costly car, and many luxuries; and I realised that I had wasted a considerable part of my life and my money. In order to escape from suffering and persecution and wanting to live an easy life I had many times compromised with the worldly standards." Dear reader how about you? Is your life also the same?

Suffering for Christ's sake should be viewed as a privilege. Nothing great was ever done without much enduring – Catherine.

Let us learn to pray:

Lord, help me to see the sunshine through the
rain,
What I count loss may show how be gain
Help me to sing when I would cry
Knowing that thou art standing by.

What matters if this life is brief?
What matters if I've toil or grief?
I, in my Saviour, find relief
Of all my joy, He is the chief.
God reigns! I will be true.

So we need to be faithful in our Private life,
Public life, Penny life, Priestly calling and in
Persecution. Let us totally pour out our lives at
the altar and be faithful servants of God. In
closing, I would like you to join with me in the
prayer of the Acua Indian Martyr, **Jim Eliot**,
"God, I pray Thee, light these idle sticks of my
life, and may I burn for Thee. Consume my life,
my God, for it is Thine. I seek not a long life,
but a full one like You, Lord Jesus."

Chapter - 5
Faithfulness in Husband-Wife Relationship

In family relationship, three words are almost as powerful as the famous "I Love You." The words are: "Maybe you're right." Marriage is one of the most intimate and difficult of human relationships. It is not to be leaped into, but entered with deliberate and solemn steps. It is infinitely rewarding at its best and unspeakably oppressive at its worst. Faithfulness in family relationships primarily refers to commitment to one another. Let us try to understand this commitment between members of a Christian family.

Deep

Too many people marry for better or worse, but not for good. When a pastor asked, "Do you take this man for better or worse?" the bride replied, "He can't become worse any more or any better, so I take him as he is." Marriage is a unique human relationship with a deepening and expanding experience. It needs plenty of give and take if it is to survive. If one partner constantly gives while the other does only taking, then it is a possessive and unhealthy relationship. A satisfying marriage relationship does not come naturally. Both the husband and wife should faithfully fulfil the unique responsibilities given to them in the Bible.

Distinct

The Bible places distinct demands upon the husband. He has a very unique position in marriage. He stands in the Christian family as the representative of Christ and is called to love his wife like him **(Eph. 5:23-30).** And how did Christ love the Church? He came from heaven's glory to be the servant and demonstrated the ultimate form of love — giving oneself.

Therefore, the husband's love towards his wife is to be expressed in loving service in her behalf and giving unto her, as unto the weaker vessel **(1 Pet. 3:7),** rather than demanding and commanding her submission. Husbands must recognize that their wives occupy a place of honour in the home. Every husband should judge his love for his wife nothing less than the sacrifice of his own best interests for her best interests.

Direct

Paul very clearly instructs husbands not to be bitter and harsh **(Col. 3:19).** He should respect and honour her and feel free to share with her his deep feelings without secretly holding anything to himself. He must tactfully communicate with her, explaining why he is having difficulty, and asking for her help and co-operation. He should not hold her failures and wrong actions against her, since love keeps no record of wrongs **(1 Cor. 13:5)**. He should directly address her on family matters and issues.

1

Conflict between husband and wife not only affects the spiritual atmosphere of the home but their physical health too. Doctors say that husband-wife fighting produces rheumatoid arthritis in women because of resentment, and peptic ulcers in men because of emotional upsets. Issues need to be sorted out through sharing and caring.

Voluntary

Many wives find it difficult either to accept or appreciate the concept of submission mentioned in **Eph. 5:22, 24; 1 Pet. 3:1** and **Col. 3:18**. Here, Paul and Peter are talking about a voluntary submission, which flows from love and respect for the husband. It is self-subordination and has nothing to do with individual worth or basic equality. It is her Christian duty and is according to the will of God. The Scripture clearly indicates that this submission is mandatory, not optional and is to be continuous. It is to be done "as unto the Lord" **(Eph. 5:22)**.

Refusal to submit to the husband is therefore rebellion against God Himself. The wife then must look upon her submission to her husband as an act of love and obedience to Christ and not merely to her husband **(Jn. 14:15).**

Complementary

To be more specific, a wife's submission is a spiritual matter because it should be performed in the power of Holy Spirit. The context in which submission is commanded indicates that it can be performed only by women cleansed by the blood of Christ and who have yielded themselves to the total control of the **(Eph. 1:1-5:21; 1 Pet. 1:1-3:6)** Holy Spirit of God. **Bill Gothard** defines this submission as, "The freedom to be creative under divinely appointed authority."

God designed woman to be a complementary partner to man **(Gen. 2:18).** Submission means that she sees herself as a part of her husband's team. She can have her own ideas, opinions, desires, requests and insights. But she should lovingly make them known to her husband because in any good team, the leader makes the final decisions and plan.

Submission does not mean that the wife is inferior to her husband. The Hebrew word for helper in **Genesis 2:18** is used in Scriptures often to describe God as being man's help **(Ps. 33:20).** Just as God is the head of Christ and yet Christ and God are equals, so it is with husband and wife. Therefore, being a wife is a dignified, responsible and honourable position.

A Christian wife should find her great joy and satisfaction in willing subjection to her husband out of love. The wife's submission should come with a realization that at last her heart has found its rest.

2

Healthy

The husband and wife should be faithful to each other in thoughts, words, motives and action. We are accountable to God for our unhealthy thoughts we think about our spouse. We need to exercise ourselves to keep our thoughts pure and clean, share openly with each other without having any secret thoughts about the other. Are the words that come out of our lips true to our conscience? It is not right to hide bitterness in our hearts towards each other and speak out with sugar-coated words. He who conceals hatred has lying lips **(Prov. 10:18).**

We must also be faithful to each other in our motives and actions. There is a possibility that we can do the right things with the wrong motives. Sometimes we can help, support, be good, or talk lovingly to each other with a wrong motive of some personal security or gain.

So, we should always judge our motives and keep them open to the conviction and correction of the Holy Spirit of God. More than anything, the husband and wife should be faithful to each other in sexual thoughts and actions. This is an area where even many Christian couples have failed. Marriage is a sacrament of love and grace. This love is sealed by sexuality and sexuality in turn needs this love to function with integrity. This love should keep the spouses loyal and faithful to each other.

Chapter - 6
Faithfulness in the Parent - Child Relationship

Five-year-old Susan said to the lady next door, "I don't think mummy knows how to bring up children, because she makes me go to bed when I am not sleepy, and wakes me up when I am sleeping."

Little Suresh asked his mother, "Why must I always take a nap when you are tired?"

Rejected by the college of his liking, a young boy angrily told his father, "If you really cared, for me you would have pulled some wires." "I know," replied the father sadly, "To begin with, I should have first pulled the wires of the TV, video, stereo and the telephone."

1. Things That Influence Children

Children cannot immediately or easily understand the motive behind certain actions of parents. Hence the parents should have a heart to heart chat with them about things concerning them. Parents should make them understand that all they do is out of love and concern for them.

Children are affected the most by the things they see and hear at home. If a child lives:

"With criticism, he learns to condemn; with hostility he learns to fight; with fear, he learns to be apprehensive; with tolerance, he learns to be patient; with encouragement, he learns to be confident; with praise he learns to be appreciative; with acceptance, he learns to love, with honesty he learns what truth is; with fairness, he learns justice; with security, he learns to have faith in himself and those about him." (Sinai Sentry)

2. The Responsibility Of The Parents

The Bible says, "Fathers do not provoke your children to anger, but bring them up in the discipline and instruction of the Lord" **(Eph. 6:4)**, and again, "...Do not exasperate your children, that they may not lose heart." **(Col. 3:21).** David Wilkerson said, "Every word and deed of a parent is a fiber woven into the character of a child, which ultimately determines how that child fits into the fabric of society."

A teen-age girl told her friend that she gets "A" grade in French because her parents were born in Paris and speak French at home. Her friend's reply to this was, "In that case, I should be getting "A" in geometry, because my parents are often square and talk in circles."

3. The Role of Christian Parents

We see below what children expect their parents to be:

C   Cheerful, courageous, a church-goer.
H   Hopeful, honest, helpful, hospitable, humble.
R   Reverent, responsible, righteous, reliable.
I   Industrious, informed, inspiring.
S   Sincere, slow to anger, shares with others, serene
T   Tolerant, temperate.
I   Instrument for God, increasing in grace.
A   Alert, appreciative.
N   Neighbourly, never coveting or gossiping.

P   Patient, practical, prayerful life.
A   Affectionate, approachable.
R   Religious, reasonable, relaxed.
E   Enthusiastic, even - tempered.
N   Not nudging others, never breaking a promise.
T   Trust worthy, thankful, tactful.

4. Children Regard Parents As Their Model

A child's concept of God is built on his know-ledge of his own earthly father and his relation-ship with him. If we want our children to think of God as their Heavenly Father, then it is important that we parents should be a model of this Heavenly Father, Who is unconditionally loving **(Rom. 5:8)**, is patient and repeatedly forgiving **(Ps. 103:8)**, is always ready to listen **(1 Pet. 3:12)**, provides for the needs of His children **(Philip. 4:19)**, provides us with security, comfort, and encouragement **(Ps. 91:4)**, lives a holy life **(Lev. 11:44)**, is prepared to make a personal sacrifice for His children **(2 Cor. 8:9)**, is fair and just, punishes with love **(Deut. 32:4)** is steadfast, un-wavering **(Mal. 3:6)**, teaches and guides **(Ps. 32:8)**, desires His best for us, delights in the company, presence and fellowship of His children **(Prov. 8:31)**, is slow to speak and slow to anger **(James 1:19)**, and speaks the truth in love **(Eph. 4:15).**

5. Children Demand Your Time

More than anything else children value the time parents spend with them. One percent of the child's time is spent in Sunday school, 7 percent in public school and 92 percent at home. Enough time should be given for listening, understanding helping and guiding them in their daily activities. If you want your children to have a fruitful future, spend twice as much time with them, and half as much money.

Children do not think much of the past or worry about their future, but are eager to experience and enjoy the present. Many parents say, everything they are engaged in for the present - earning money, saving, and building a house - is to ensure a good future for their children. They fail to understand that children evaluate their parents' love and affection for them in terms of time spent with them today and not money or material spent or saved for them.

Children start to roam, when parents don't stay home. Parents tend to concentrate more on the future financial benefits for the children rather than spending time in bringing them up in the fear of the Lord. Considering the number of divorces today, it seems that more parents are running away from home than children. Our children are the only earthly possessions we can take with us to the glorious heaven. Visualize your children as lovely little two-legged walking computers whom we can programme into the Biblical path of life, by teaching them the word of God and praying for them. If children are to find the way to God, parents must point the way.

Chapter - 7
Faithfulness in Pain and Suffering

Paul talks about the credentials of his apostolic commission in **2 Corinthians 11:22-27.** He boasts about his weakness and says that he delights in infirmities, in reproaches, in persecutions, and in distressing circumstances for the sake of Christ. He talks about his thorn in the flesh in **2 Corinthians 12:7-10.**

Many have guessed about the identity of this "Splinter in the flesh." Whatever it was, it was probably the "Bodily ailment" from which he suffered when he first visited the Galatians. He received an answer for his thrice-repeated prayer for the removal of this sickness, not by his deliverance from it, but by his receiving the necessary grace to bear it - not simply to live with it, but to be thankful for it. If his ministry was so effective in spite of this physical weakness, then the transcendent power was not his own, but from God.

1. Our Weakness is Essential for God's Power

We need to recognise that our weaknesses are not barriers to God's power, but instead encourages us to look forward to avail that power. Paul said, "*I will boast of the things that show my weakness.*" **(2 Cor. 11:30).** Our weakness opens the way for us to experience the superabundant strength of God's grace.

In fact, God gives strength to go through affliction. When we are strong in ourselves, sometimes we hinder His power. So in a way our weakness is essential for God's power to work in us.

Paul did not glory in the infirmities themselves, but because through his infirmities Christ had opportunity to manifest His power more effectively. Paul could rejoice in his personal weakness, in deprivations of food, drink, and money, in persecutions and in all the troubles related to his ministry because he had the assurance that the grace of God was operating through him.

For this reason Paul had a healthy attitude towards life. Cheerfully he pressed forward toward the goal **(Philip. 3:12).**

The fact that Paul's, *"thorn in the flesh"* was not removed does not mean that God cannot or will not heal those who call on Him, nor does it mean that He will necessarily send suffering to those He calls to serve Him. He deals with each person on an individual basis. He will make His grace sufficient for us. Our weaknesses are not handicaps in our service; they are vehicles of God's loving sufficiency. God proved to Paul that no matter what his weakness was, His strength was sufficient.

Someone said to a humble Christian woman, rich toward God, "Are you the woman with the great faith?" "Oh, no," said she; "I am the woman with a little faith in a great God!"

2. Knocked Down, But Never Knocked Out

Paul talks about receiving **39** lashes five times from the Jews in **2 Corinthians 11:24.** The maximum number of lashes prescribed by the written law was forty **(Deut. 25:3).** On the principle of "Setting a hedge around the law," to prevent its accidental transgression, it was traditionally restricted to thirty-nine. **(Mishnah Makkot 3:10-15).**

Thrice he was beaten with rods. In the Lystra riot, Paul was badly knocked about; and, years later, he says to his friends in Corinth, "Once I was stoned" **(2 Cor. 11:25).** He must have been knocked unconscious, for those who stoned him dragged him out of the city, supposing that he was dead. But as the new converts gathered around to see what could be done for him, consciousness returned and he went back into the city with them **(Acts 14:19,20)**. Whatever his physical disabilities

were, Paul had an extraordinarily tough and
resilient constitution and remarkable staying
power. "He was often knocked down, but never
knocked out." **(2 Cor. 4:9)**. He speaks of
bearing on his body *the marks of Jesus* - the
stigmata that indicated who his master was,
just as slaves sometimes had their owner's
name branded in their flesh **(Gal. 6:17).**

3. Paul's Theology of Pain and Suffering

Paul's theology was not based on experiences
which might be described as mystical, it is
based on Jesus, the fulfiller of God's promise
and purpose of salvation; Jesus, the crucified
and exalted Lord; Jesus, the divine wisdom, in
whom God creates, maintains and brings to
consummation everything that exists; Jesus
who, here and now, lives within his people by
His spirit.

Paul was thrust into the Lord's ministry with a
promise of suffering and not with the promise
of a bed of roses. He says, "The Holy Spirit
solemnly testifies to him in every city saying
that bonds and afflictions await him." **(Acts
20:23).** Thrice he suffered shipwreck, a night
and a day and had been in the deep.

No one can live a Christian life without
suffering. If a so called Christian comes to me
and says that he has no problems whatsoever,

then I would have the problem of believing that he is a Christian. There is something basically wrong in him. He must have been a compromiser and not an overcomer.

As sinners we are called to be saved. As saints we are called to suffer. "But if any one suffers as a Christian, he is not to be ashamed, but is to glorify God in this name." **(I Pet. 4:16).** Christ always associated together His sufferings and His glorification.

Without the Cross, there is no Crown. Cross bearing ends in crown wearing. Jesus was pierced through for our transgressions. He was crushed for our iniquities; the chastening for our well-being fell upon him. "Surely our griefs He Himself bore, and our sorrows He carried..." **(Is. 53:4,5).**

During the war in London - a Pastor walking along the street said to a wounded British soldier, "Thank you for being wounded for me," and then further added, "... I know some one who was wounded for you."

Jesus emptied Himself, suffered for us and endured to the extent of a shameful, painful death on the cross for our sake. Is it not our responsibility to honour His sufferings and be willing and ready to suffer for His cause? That is what Paul says, in **Philip. 3:7,8,10** "I have counted [everything] as loss for the sake of Christ... so that I may gain Christ... that I may know Him and the power of His resurrection and the fellowship of His sufferings, being conformed to His death." When we have left this life we shall not have a second chance of bearing the cross of Christ - **Sadhu Sunder Singh.**

4. In The Storms of Life

Paul's long list of problems and suffering speaks of the struggle in which he had been engaged in order to carry the Gospel of Christ to the world. He actually accepted hardships as normal experiences, rather than exceptional **(2 Cor. 11:23-33).**

"Labours," probably refers to the physical work he did in order to support himself. "Stripes," speaks of the beatings he received as a violator of the Jewish law. Five of his "imprisonments" are recorded in Acts. The "shipwrecks" must have been part of earlier journeys, before **Acts 27.** The expression, "deaths of" indicates that his life was frequently threatened. Paul had to travel almost constantly, and was often in danger of floods and robbers. Three times he went through shipwrecks.

What to do when the ship is sinking?

Jesus was sleeping when the ship was sinking. A great windstorm arose, and the waves beat into the boat, so that it was already filling. But Jesus was in the stern, asleep on a pillow. And they awoke Him and said to Him, "'Teacher, do you not care that we are perishing?' And He got up and rebuked the wind and said to the sea, 'Hush, be still.' And the wind died down and it became perfectly calm. And He said to them, 'Why are you afraid? Do you still have no faith?' They became very much afraid and said to one another, 'Who then is this, that even the wind and the sea obey Him?'" **(Mk. 4:35-41; see also Matt. 8:23-27; Lk. 8:22-25).**

At times of difficulty we learn more about the Lord. This was the experience of the disciples. This miracle becomes an illustration of the truth that even the Disciples of Christ may go through difficult situations that cause fear and anxiety.

Often it is only in the storms of life that believers experience the power of God. It is that power that takes care of our problems. Sometimes, money and experience cannot save us, as in the instance of this storm. We are forced to come to the end of all human resources before we are willing to experience the power of God.

The skill of those expert seamen, their knowledge of the lake, and their past experiences as sailors were of no use. In their anxiety the disciples were even questioning whether the Lord cared for them. But he did, and he does. Peter learned the lesson that night well, for later he wrote, "...He cares for you." (**1 Peter 5:7**, where the same word for "care" is used as in the accounts of this miracle). What a great comfort it is to know that an all-powerful Saviour cares for us with an infinitely gracious love!

Jesus was fast asleep in the midst of dashing waves and drenching storm. How could He do that? No doubt He was a true man, but a man of true faith in His heavenly Father.
David could lie down and sleep when he had enemies wanting to kill him. He says, "I lay down and slept; I awoke, for the Lord sustains me. I will not be afraid of ten thousands of people who have set themselves against me round about." **(Ps. 3:5,6).** Peter was fast asleep in the dungeons of king Herod till the angel of deliverance wakes him up, though he knew that death was awaiting him **(Acts 12:6).**

There were also dangers created by hostile people. But external perils were not the thing; Paul also underwent other strains, weariness, painfulness, hunger and thirst, fasting, cold and nakedness. The burden of the churches weighed him down - the heresy of Galatia, the confusion in Thessalonica, the immorality in Corinth. All of these were part of the burden he carried continually in his heart.

Our distresses are not necessarily an indication of God's disfavour. If that were the case, then one would be forced to conclude that Paul was out of the will of the Lord when he suffered want **(Philip. 4:12)**. Our disappointments are God's appointments.

God has not promised His children physical comfort, material prosperity, or freedom from persecution, though we live in a dispensation of grace. He has blessed us with all spiritual blessings **(Eph. 1:3)**, and He has promised to supply all our material need **(Philip. 4:19)**, but physical comfort may not necessarily be the material need. Suffering and difficulty may well be expected to characterize a normal Christian experience.

This condition is what Paul meant when he said that as believers we might expect suffering: "For your sake we are being put to death all day long; we are considered as sheep to be slaughtered." **(Rom. 8:36; 1 Pet. 1:6-7).**

Paul recalls a humiliating experience. "In Damascus the ethnarch under Aretas the king was guarding the city of the Damascenes in order to seize me, and I was let down in a basket through a window in the wall, and so escaped his hands." **(2 Cor. 11:32, 33).**

Paul did not boast of his achievements, nor of the hardships he had willingly suffered for the sake of Christ. The scars that his experiences left he wears with pride: they were the indelible stigmata that proclaimed him to be the bond slave of the Lord in whose service he had received them.

Jesus was all-human. He had the same pain as you and I would have. The agony was so great that He even went to the extent of praying, "Father if Thou art willing remove this cup from Me, yet not My will, but Thine be done."

Don't worry if you are shedding tears today because of your stand for Christ. One day, He shall wipe away every tear from your eyes, and there shall no longer be any mourning, crying, or pain, for the first things will have passed away **(Rev. 21:4)**. The Lord God will remove the reproach of His people from all the earth. This is the Lord for whom we have waited, let us rejoice and be glad in His salvation **(Is. 25:8, 9)**. God shall wipe every tear from your eyes **(Rev. 7:16, 17)**. God will take care of what you go through, but you must take care of how you go through it.

Chapter - 8
Faithfulness in Our Attitudes

An attitude is an emotional and motivational force towards a psychological object. Some times we try to picture attitude as 'value,' 'belief' or 'opinion.' Attitude is different from them. Belief is its cognitive base, and action its cognitive side. In fact, attitude is part of the broad value system. We value something depending on our beliefs and attitudes.

Belief is a thought process, which includes a clear perception of value. We form an opinion based on our beliefs and attitudes. But attitudes keep changing with the onset of new environmental influences.

1. The Nature and Choice of Attitude

Nicolo Paganini, a very famous, gifted violinist, was playing through a difficult piece of music to a packed audience. A full orchestra surrounded him with magnificent support. Suddenly, one string of his violin snapped and hung down from his violin. Though he was shocked and was perspiring, he continued to play the music beautifully.

To the conductor's surprise, a second string broke, and in a short time, a third one broke; now, there were three limping strings dangling from Nicolo's violin, but still, the expert performer completed the difficult composition on the one remaining string.

The audience jumped to its feet and shouted "Bravo! Bravo!" As the applause was over, the violinist asked the people to sit back down. He held the violin high for everyone to see and signaled at the conductor to begin the orchestra and he placed the violin beneath his chin and played the final piece on one string as the audience and the conductor shook their heads in silent amazement. This can be called as an attitude of fortitude - Paganini and one string! We must have this kind of perseverance. What is perseverance? It means, firstly, to take hold; secondly, to hold on; thirdly, and lastly, never to let go.

The longer we live, the more we become convinced that life is **10%** what happens to us and **90%** how we respond to it. We are more than what happens to us. We should never forget the fact that people are constantly watching us. They are watching our reactions more than our actions. A man or a woman of God should not react but only lovingly respond. How do we respond to our life situations? We respond as we interpret the meaning of actions upon us.

Dr. Victor Frankel was a bold, courageous Jew who endured years of indignity and humiliation as a prisoner of the Nazis. In the beginning of their trials, he was brought into the courtroom. His captors had taken away his home and family, his cherished freedom, his possessions, even his watch and wedding ring.

They had shaved his head and stripped his clothing off his body. He was interrogated and falsely accused. He was destitute, a helpless pawn in the hands of brutal, prejudiced, sadistic men. For all practical purposes, there was nothing that he could do. But suddenly, Dr. Frankel realized that, he still had the power to choose his own attitude. No matter what anyone would ever do to him, regardless of what the future held for him, the attitude of choice was his to make. He could either hold on to his bitter feelings or change to forgiveness, to give up or to continue, hatred or hope, determination to endure or the paralysis of self-pity. It boiled down to Frankel and one string!

In reality, we must admit that we spend more of our time concentrating and fretting over the strings that snap, dangle and pop - the things that cannot be changed - than we do giving attention to the one that remains, our choice of attitude.

An attitude can be defined as an organization of interrelated beliefs around a common object, or a situation with certain aspects being at the focus of attention for some people and the other aspects for others. Belief is its cognitive base, and action its cognitive side. All beliefs are predisposition to action. Each belief within an attitude organization is conceived to have three components such as cognitive, affective and behavioral.

A cognitive component represents a person's knowledge about what is good or bad, true or false, desirable or undesirable. An affective component takes a positive or a negative position with respect to the object of belief when its validity is seriously questioned, as in an argument. The kind of action a behavioral component leads to is dictated strictly by the content of the belief. Jastrow has pointed out that the human mind is a belief seeking rather than a fact-seeking apparatus.

Virtually all theories agree that an attitude is not a basic irreducible element within the personality, but represents a cluster or syndrome of two or more interrelated elements. Someone said, "A person's social behaviour is mediated by at least two types of attitudes - one activated by the object, the other by the situation." A person's opinion is a verbal expression of his belief, attitude, or value. The

concept of sentiment is more or less synony-
mous with attitude.

Certain environmental influences produce
certain attitudes and hence these may not
remain steady but change with the develop-
ment of new environmental influences. The
change may take place consciously or uncon-
sciously.

It is imperative that we consider the impact of
our attitudes towards the complexities of our
life situations in the following chapters.

2. Attitude Towards Irritation

We need to consider the reality of our reactions
to irritations. Some of our common irritants
are: traffic jams, long queues, crying babies,
misplaced keys, nosy and noisy neighbours,
peeling onions, flat tires, all the in-laws and
outlaws including the mothers-in-law and the
daughters-in-law.

The secret of overcoming irritation lies in
adjusting. There is a three fold truth in adjust-
ing: (i) I can change no other person by direct
action; (ii) I can change only myself; (iii) When
I change, others tend to change in response to
that. In this regard, we can learn a great lesson
from the oyster and its pearl. Pearls are the
product of pain. For some unknown reason, the

shell of the Oyster gets pierced and an alien substance, a grain of sand slips inside. On the entry of that foreign irritant, all the resources within the tiny, sensitive oyster rush to the spot and begin to release healing fluids that otherwise would have remained idle. By and by, the irritant is covered and the wound is healed, leading to the formation of a pearl. No other gem seems as precious as pearl in the history of this world. It is the symbol of stress—a healed wound—a precious tiny jewel conceived through irritation, born of adversity, nursed by adjustments. Had there been no wounding, no irritating interruption, there could have been no pearl.

Some oysters are never wounded, and those who seek for pearl toss them aside, fit only for stew curry. The Bible says, "When all kinds of trials crowd into your lives, my brothers don't resent them as intruders, but welcome them as friends. Realize that they have come to test your endurance. But let the progress go on until the endurance is fully developed, and you will find you have become men and women of mature character" **(Jas. 1:2, 3 J.B. Phillips)**.

You must learn to be patient in stressful situations, otherwise you will become a patient. In order to keep mole hills of tensions from becoming mountains of stress you can develop certain precautionary measures such as (i)

Allow for a margin of error, (ii) Put things in perspective, (iii) Plan for delays, (iv) Think ahead, (v) Be prepared even for the worst, and (vi) Live for the moment.

3. Attitude of Blaming Others

This is an aggressive attitude that reacts to circumstances with blame. Most of the time, we blame others for our failures and the blunders we have committed. Sometimes we even tend to blame God. Blaming is a system of avoiding responsibility. We have an impulse to blame because it promises an escape. Spiritual growth and maturity comes to a Christian only by owning responsibility and working at resolving it.

We should have no excuses for our failures, and no escapes for our mistakes. This is precisely the way to minimize our failures and cut down on our mistakes. Even if some one else is at fault, the responsibility of a Christian is to kindly and lovingly exhort that person, showing much concern for that person and his back-ground and life situation. The most powerful rebuke is not a loud, negative blast, but a quiet, positive model.

We are not going to achieve anything by blaming others. Blame never affirms; it trau-matizes. Blame never heals; it hurts. Blame never solves;

it complicates. Blame never forgives; it rejects. Blame never unites; it separates. Blame never builds; it breaks. Blame never smiles; it frowns. Blame never comforts; it disturbs. Let us admit that until we stop blaming others, we will never enjoy health and happiness again. Rather, if we own up to the mess we are in, there is hope for us, and we will receive help.

4. Attitude of Rationalization

Rationalization is a dangerous attitude which has been corrupting the lives of many common people as well as leaders. The dictionary defines rationalizing as, "Providing plausible, but untrue, reasons for conduct." In other words, it is what we do when we substitute untrue explanations for true reasons. One sin, when rationalized, becomes two.

Sometimes we cloud our actual motives with a smoke screen of excuses that sound very nice. There is much difference between good sound reasons and reasons that sound good. Often we do this to justify ourselves in the eyes of others. Rationalization is a mental technique which allows you to be unfair to others without feeling guilty. Sometimes rationalization causes people to gloss over open and obvious sin.

So the principle is, if you're wrong in what you are doing, humbly accept it and stop doing it.

No amount of rationalization will make it right or convince anyone. If you are sure what you are doing is right and not in any way a contradiction to the Word of God, and if your conscience is clear, then relax and be bold to express yourself with confidence. The main thing is that you please the Lord with a clear conscience.

5. Attitude of Self-Pity

"Self-pity is when you begin to feel that no man's land is your island," said Dana Robins. Self-pity makes you to be absorbed in yourself and you are fascinated by your own egos. You need to understand that the world was not created for you personally, and that it is your pride and self-centeredness that lies at the root of your problems. "Self pity is a prison without walls—a sign pointing to nowhere".
— Anonymous

Take your eyes off yourself. When "I" is put to death, the Spirit of Christ can control your life and make it beautiful. It is as addictive as alcohol—and just as deadly.

Despair and Discouragement

Self-pity is always counter-productive. It is destructive. If continued, it will lead to discouragement, which in turn is often the most direct route to despair and the ultimate self-destruction—suicide.

We should not become prisoners of ourselves. When doors are slammed against us, we are prone to draw into ourselves. Distrust begets distrust. Perhaps some people have lost faith in themselves because they feel God is far away from them. We must trust God where we cannot trace him.

Deliverance from Depression

The body and the will have their part to play in mastering mental depression. Hence, the first step is to get out of the depressed situation. Some effort on the depressed is called for. The old maxim, "You never know what you can do till you try," still holds well. The ability and the will to try are made largely out of past efforts that have brought good results. Surprisingly, time and again we have completed tasks, which we first thought were beyond our capability.

The second step is to look up. We need to look beyond what we can accomplish in our own strength with a positive attitude.

Counter Crisis with Courage

Courage has to be sustained by the encourage-
ment of others. Courage is the keystone in the
sustenance of our character. We should have
the boldness to stand for the right, honesty and
justice. In times of crisis, we need the attitude
of fortitude to keep us from being overcome
when things run over us.

God Is Never Off Duty

Hence, the best thing would be to rest in peace,
re-evaluate your life and spend your time in
prayer and meditation upon the word of God.
Never allow self-pity to overtake you. In
essence, self-pity is a bitter resentment of one's
condition and an attempt to get back on others
or to manipulate others into giving (showing)
sympathy.

If you are a person entangled in self-pity, and
would like to come out of it, try to do the
following: think about the positive and negative
things in your life. Can anything good come out
of my illness or problems? Can I get a much
broader and realistic view of the present
situation? How can I make the best use of this
situation?

There are many such attitudes we should take
care of. In which areas do we face our greatest

struggles? For example are we more often negative than positive? Or are we stubborn and closed rather than open and willing to hear? Is our attitude toward people very different from us? Are we proud and prejudiced? I would like to exhort us through the words of Paul who said, "Have this attitude in yourselves which was also in Christ Jesus, who... emptied Himself, taking the form of a bond-servant..." **(Philip. 2:5-7)**. May the Lord help us to exercise the attitude of servant-hood like Jesus.

Therefore, the single, most significant decision you can make on a day-to-day basis is your choice of attitude. It is the 'single string' that keeps you going or cripples your progress. "It alone fuels your desires or assaults your hope," says, Charles Swindoll. When your attitudes are right, there is no barrier too high, no valley too deep, no dream too extreme, and no challenge too great for you.

Chapter - 9
Faithfulness in Our Prayer Life

The people who have done the most for God are those who have prayed the most. I am sure any person considered to be a great man or woman would definitely be a great prayer warrior in his or her personal life.

ABRAHAM prayed; his son was born.
ELIEZER prayed; Rebecca appeared.
JOSEPH prayed; his brothers were changed.
MOSES prayed; heaven's wrath was subdued.
JOSHUA prayed; Ai was destroyed.
HANNAH prayed; Samuel was given.
ELIJAH prayed; the heavens shut and opened, and fire came from above.
ELISHA prayed; a dead child came back to life.
DAVID prayed; Goliath was slain.
DANIEL prayed; the mouths of lions were shut, and archangels were set in motion.
JESUS prayed; the pillars of the church were chosen.
DISCIPLES prayed; the Holy Spirit came upon them.
THE CHURCH prayed; Peter was released from the prison.
It was PERSISTENT prayer, PREVAILING prayer, and PINPOINTED prayer.

What Is Prayer?

Prayer is the declaration of a believer's faith in God and in His promises. It is an act of expressing our faith in Him. The world seeks victory by trying to get back on its feet, but the Christians by going down on their knees. Leonard Raven Hill writes, "Poverty stricken as the church is today in many things, she is most stricken in the place of prayer." Today, many people try to come into the limelight of the spiritual circle and very soon they are found like flat tires, because there is no backing of prayers in their lives. Very little importance is given for prayer in our churches. There are many organisers, but few agencies; many players, but few prayers; many singers, but few clingers; lots of pastors, but few wrestlers; many fears, but few tears; much fashion, but little passion; many interpreters, but few intercessors; many writers, but few fighters.

The church is becoming poor in terms of prayer. If people are invited for a healing crusade, thousands would probably come. But if it is for an evangelistic meeting, few hundreds would come and when we call for a prayer meeting, only a very few would. It is commonly said, "Today, it's only a prayer meeting, and not a special meeting." That's why there is no power in our lives. In the true sense, prayer is to be given the greatest and the utmost importance in our lives.

The current trend is that when we pray it is like taking a market list to God. We have a long list - 1 kilo potato, 1/2 kilo of tomato, 1 kilo rice etc. You may call it supplication. The Bible says, 'Go before your God with prayer and supplications.' We make application and then supplications, and that is the main part of our prayers. If you happen to record your prayers and play it back, 90 per cent of your prayers are about your problems or you can hear the phrases like, 'gimme, Lord,' 'gimme, gimme, gimme; I am Jimmy, Lord!' There are many 'gimme Jimmys' in the spiritual circle. This is not prayer, but supplication.

Prayer is the key that unlocks all the store houses of God's infinite grace and power. All that God is, and all that God has is at the disposal of prayer. There is an unlimited amount of power and authority available with God. But we need to receive it through our earnest prayers. There are no barriers for the believer who knows how to pray and who meets all the conditions of prevailing prayer. An old Jewish mystic says, "Prayer is the moment when heaven and earth kiss each other." Bring the heaven to come, and kiss the earth through your prayers.

The secret of prayer is not what you do or how you do it, for God knows our needs, even before we ask. Actually, prayer is nothing more than opening up the lines of communication, establishing rapport, and removing the roadblocks between God and you.

How To Pray So As To Get What You Ask

One of the most powerful prayers in the Bible is in **Acts 12:5**, "...but prayer for him was being made fervently by the church to God." This is the record of a most remarkable prayer in the Bible. King Herod had killed James, the brother of John. This greatly pleased the Jews. So he proceeded further to arrest the leader of the whole Apostolic Company, the Apostle Peter, with the intention of killing him also. But the arrest was during the Passover week, the holy week of the Jews, and though the Jews were perfectly willing to have him assassinated they were not willing to have their holy week desecrated by his death. So Peter was cast into prison to be kept until the Passover week was over. It was the last night of the Passover week and the next morning Peter was supposed to be brought in for trial and probably to be beheaded.

There seemed to be little hope for Peter, or no hope at all. The Christian believers in Jerusalem held a prayer meeting for Peter. So all the disciples and friends of Peter had gathered in the house of Mary, the mother of John Mark, and they prayed for Peter's release.

They did not use any other method or means to save Peter. What was happening to Peter at that time? Peter was having a sound sleep. Only a praying Christian can have sound sleep even at the time when his/her life is in danger. Perhaps, Peter was snoring after finishing his prayers. There were sixteen soldiers guarding him, and soldiers on either side who were chained to him flanked him. Seeing Peter sleep so peacefully, they, too, fell asleep. An angel appeared and woke him up saying, "Come on, get up, Peter. Get up!"

He was able to have a sound sleep because I believe he would have prayed probably like this, "Lord, no one has any authority over my life. Not a single hair of my head will fall without your permission. If you want me to come to you, I will come to you. If you want me to stay back, I will stay back. My life is in your hands. I hand over my life to you." He said, 'Goodnight, Lord' and slept. Hallelujah! We say goodnight mummy, goodnight daddy, goodnight darling, goodnight honey, and then we go to sleep, but we forget to say 'goodnight, Lord.' And if we forget to say 'goodnight, Lord,' then at midnight, Satan may say 'goodnight' to you.

If Peter was worried and did not have faith in the Lord, neither he nor the soldiers would have slept and the angel might not have come, or even if the angel had released him, the soldiers could have arrested him again. Many times our worry or unbelief is the hindrance for God to perform miracles in our lives. Jesus questions, "Which of you, by taking thought can add one cubit to his stature?" **(Matt. 6:25 KJV)**. Stop worrying and hand over your problem to the Lord and say, 'Lord, this is not my problem; it's yours.' The battle is the Lord's, the victory is mine. Perhaps Peter believed this, and hence he slept peacefully.

An angel from the Lord woke him up and the iron chains broke and fell down. There is another miracle in this passage. We must analyse when we study the Bible. When the iron chains fall down, they make noise and the soldiers can be woken because of the sound. But God took care of that. The iron chains never made a noise. When you pray to God, he takes care of every single detail of your problem. You don't have to tell God, 'God be careful when you are doing that miracle; the iron chain is going to make a noise.' He knows everything. Some people try to explain to God all that they want. We need to just relax and hand over the entire problem to him. Most of the time after we pray, we try to manipulate the situation. In that case, God can never do a miracle in your life.

After that, we read the story of how Peter was led out, and he arrived at the house of Mary, the mother of Mark. Peter knew very well that, it was a house of prayer and that his fellow believers would be praying for him. He knocked at the door. There was a little servant girl named Rhoda praying along with others. The moment she heard the knock she sprang to her feet and rushed to the gate, perhaps, saying to herself, 'That must be Peter' or probably she would have asked, "Is that Peter?" When she recognized his voice she was so excited that she even forgot to open the door and dashed back to tell the group about Peter's arrival. But they just could not believe it. Peter was still knocking and finally they opened the gate and there he was! Peter stood at the doorstep, as a living evidence of God's answer to their prayer.

It is amazing to notice that among all those who were praying, only Rhoda was mentioned by name in the Bible. It is purely because of her faith alone. Rhoda means 'rose' and she was indeed a rose that would be very fragrant to God, although she was only a servant girl. For, there is no sweeter fragrance to God than the fragrance of faith.

Now let us analyse how these people prayed. "...[P]rayer was made without ceasing of the church unto God for him." **(Acts 12:5 KJV)**. The whole secret of prevailing prayer is found in four phrases in this brief description of their uttered prayer: (i) "unto God" (ii) "without ceasing" (iii) "of the church" (iv) "for him." Let us now analyse them one by one.

Praying Unto God

What do we mean by 'praying unto God?' Why does it say, 'they prayed unto God?' Don't we all pray unto God? We all pray to God. *'Praying unto God'* means going into the presence of God and praying. Often when people stand up to pray in public or kneel down in private closets, they tend to think far more of what they ask for, but fail to comprehend the greatness of God who made heaven and earth and who possesses power over all things. We do take the name of God upon our lips, but there is no real conscious access to God. If we really want our prayers to be powerful, the first step is to experience the presence of God while we pray. Brother Lawrence once said, "Prayer is nothing else than a sense of God's presence." In order to achieve this first of all we need to forget and forsake everything around us and remain silent for some time until we feel the presence of God.

The best time to pray is early in the morning. He who seeks me early shall find me. So get up early in the morning and pray. What should you do early in the morning? Get up! I know you don't like to get up. Some people just want to lie down and have a horizontal meditation. They pray, 'Lord, thank you for the night's sleep and the rest you gave me,' then they snore back to sleep and then they wake up and pray again. No horizontal meditation will do. Amos says, "Woe to those who are at ease in Zion...." **(Amos 6:1)** There's no real rest for Christians. If you rest, you will rust. Get up from your bed, go to the bathroom, clean yourself up, wash your face, and brush your teeth. Please don't go to God with bad breath.

Feel fresh in the sight of God. If the President of your country calls you tonight to dine with him, how would you go? You would have on your best outfit, a suitable hairstyle, the best perfume possible and you would be fresh and clean. If you can go to a worldly authority so well prepared, how well prepared should you be in the presence of the Lord of Lords and the King of kings. We Christians, tend to have no fear of God. We take the love of God for granted. Other people seem to have more fear of their gods than Christians do. The reason, I think, Christians do not have the fear of Jesus is because Jesus does not hold a spear or a sword in His hand. Go before God with fear and trembling. If you go before God with fear and trembling, you can stand before people with power and authority. So the presence of God is very important.

I want to place before you two important spiritual disciplines: (1) do not start praying unless you have felt the presence of God. (2) Whenever you open the Bible never close it without God speaking. Because it is God's Word and it will not return back void. God is definitely speaking to you something from that portion that you are reading, but you are not waiting in His presence to listen to Him. Christian life is a life of discipline and the word 'disciple' comes from the word 'discipline.' Discipline pays dividends.

People are in a hurry to pray quickly and go to work or do other things. Somebody prayed like this, "God bless me, my wife, my son and my daughter - we four and no more." It is not we four and no more. Do not be in a hurry when you pray. Do you hurry up when you watch cricket? You don't say one, two and I'm going away now. You are sure to relax and watch, but you don't want to relax and pray. Wait for the presence of God. If you are not able to feel the presence of God, read a few verses of Psalms or Proverbs in the Bible and sing a few songs of praise and by now you must be able to feel the presence of God. If you still do not feel the presence of God, don't start praying.

Make it a discipline (practice) in your life that you will not start praying if you are unable to feel the presence of God, but that you would cry to the Lord, saying, "Lord, what is it that is hindering you from coming to me? What is there between you and me? Why am I not able to feel your presence." Cry to Him, and now God will speak to you, perhaps saying, "Hey, you husband, last night you scolded your wife and turned to the other side and slept and she turned to the other side and slept, and this morning, do you want me to come to you? No, No! I'm not a cheap God. Go say you are sorry to your wife, then you come to Me."

Are you a person, who has been watching obscene movies on television or on the Internet and been going into all sorts of hallucinations and fantasies and have ended up in a mess. Now do you expect God just to come to you as soon as you start praying?" No. Our God is a holy God. Without holiness, no one will see the Lord **(Heb. 12:14).**

You think that you are praying, and that your prayers are being heard. No, it does not just happen. First comes the conviction through the Holy Spirit of God, if there is any unconfessed sin in our hearts. Then comes the confession.

What is confession? Confession is not telling God that you have sinned. He already knows, and that is why He has given you that conviction. The word confession means agreeing with God, saying, "Yes, Lord, I have sinned." Then comes the cleansing through the blood of Jesus, and then comes the communion with God. These four C's are very important: the conviction, the confession, the cleansing and the communion with God. Once this aspect is taken care of, then you feel the presence of God and now whatever you pray, gets into the computer of God and you can be sure of getting an output. This is exactly what I mean by going into the presence of God.

How can we access the presence of God? It is only through Jesus Christ! (**Eph. 2:18**) What happens when we come into the presence of God? We read of a woman who came to Jesus in **Luke 7:37, 38**. When she came into the presence of Jesus, she did not even utter a word, but her heart was completely broken. This incident stands as a model for us to come into the presence of God with a broken heart and a need to empty ourselves at His feet.

The Lord does not despise a broken heart and a contrite spirit. If you go to God with a proud heart, He can never fill you with His grace and peace. God can fill only an empty vessel and not a vessel that is half-filled. Go before Him broken in your spirit, empty yourself, humble yourself, prostrate yourself before the living God. She came into the presence of Jesus, and she was broken. She did not know how to pray, she never opened her mouth, she never uttered a word, she never spoke anything, but she was shedding tears, and the tears were washing the feet of Jesus. Every teardrop was a confession of every sin in her life. She did not know how to pray, but she knew how to be broken at the feet of Jesus; that is going into the presence of God. He is the only one who looks at your heart and not at your worldly possessions.

My friend, your situation might look bleak. I want to tell you, 'Cheer up! The Lord is at work.' You may not see anything but darkness, but you are praying. If you love God, the Lord loves you too. The Lord has started working. He is at work and you will see the result when the light comes. Wait till dawn and you can see what the Lord has been doing in your life. The disciples were praying away in a room, but the iron chains that bound Peter broke and fell down. Is it not a miracle?

Pray Without Ceasing

Now, let us consider the second phrase of the four used in **Acts. 12:5** that contains the secret of prevailing prayer. The phrase "without ceasing" is translated from the Greek word, 'ektenos' which means "stretched-out-edly." It is the same word used in **Luke 22:44** for "being in agony." Jesus was praying fervently and His sweat was like the drops of blood falling down upon the ground. The thought that comes to my mind is our spirit being stretched out toward God, in intense earnestness of desire. This is the experience of pouring out oneself at the altar of God.

Pray United In One Spirit

Now let us look briefly at the third one of the four phrases, "of the church." United prayer delights God. There is, of course, power in the prayer of a single individual, but there is far greater power in a united prayer. Our Lord Jesus taught this same great truth in **Matt. 18:18, 19.** "Truly I say to you, whatever you bind on earth shall have been bound in heaven; and whatever you loose on earth shall have been loosed in heaven... if two of you agree on earth..." **(Matt. 18:19)**. Hence, there is power in united prayer, provided there is real unity. There should be oneness in the body of Christ, the believers. There should not be differences or hatred or an unforgiving spirit, jealousy and so on among the believers. If there is no unity, then there is no power in prayer.

Pray Specific, Particular Prayers

The fourth phrase, "for him," denotes that the offered prayer was a definite prayer for a definite person, and that is the kind of prayer God answers specifically. General prayers are generally heard. God's answer is just as definite as your prayer is. While both were imprisoned, Peter had a sound sleep and Paul sang in high spirits. The former was peaceful and the latter joyful. They had learnt to relax and rejoice, even in depressing and difficult situations. Peter knew whom he had trusted and Paul knew whom he had tasted **(1 Pet. 2:3; 2 Tim. 1:12)**.

In closing, let me call your attention to our dependence upon the Holy Spirit in all our praying. It is the Holy Spirit who enables us to really pray unto God, who leads us into the presence of God and makes God real to us. It is the Holy Spirit again who gives us the intense earnestness in prayer that prevails with God. Still again it is the Holy Spirit who brings us into unity so that we know the power of real united prayer. And it is the Spirit who shows us the definite things for which we should definitely pray. To sum it all up, the prayer that God answers is the prayer that is offered to God the Father, that is on the ground of the atoning blood of God the Son and that is under the direction and in the power of God the Holy Spirit.

Chapter - 10
Faithfulness of a Firewood Christian

Everything that touches man concerns the church. The modern church succumbs to the worldly pattern by allowing secular thinking to reduce it to a specialized fellowship of worship, rather than being a committed community shaped by its life in Christ. Today, our churches do not reflect Jesus, and therefore, do not interpret him. Someone said, "It is not our claim, as the truth which is absolute, but the claim of the truth on us." The church cannot incarnate God, unless it is willing to go to the cross, to walk an extra mile emptying itself of all pretensions in the ultimate sacrifice which alone makes its incarnation convincing."

1. Upper Room or Supper Room

We need to learn much from the early church. Someone said, "The early church prayed in the upper room, but the present church cooks in the supper room." Much time is given for feasting and playing rather than fasting and praying. We see more people with full stomachs, but not with broken hearts, bent knees and wet eyes. There is more fire in the kitchen range than in the pulpit. The early church was filled with the Holy Ghost, not stuffed with stew and roast. Shall we put out the cooking squad and bring in the praying band, spend little time to cook and more time in the Book? Let us dine fewer dinners, but win more sinners. The trouble with many Christians today is that they would rather be on the judgment seat than on the witness stand.

2. Ideology or Theology

The church at present is a broken sign, divided not only by doctrinal controversies, but also by the same forces of caste, colour and creed that split the human community. It finds itself in a situation analogous to its early days in the Roman Empire, confronting powerful ideologies beyond its own boundaries. Today, we are troubled less by golden calves than by graven image theologies.

3. The Church That Cares

The greatest need of today is the church that cares, that heals the lives that are hurt, that comforts old people, that challenges youth, that knows no division of culture or class, no frontiers, geographical or social. It should be a working church, a worshiping church and a winsome church. It should be a church that interprets the truth in terms of the truth.

4. The Church On Fire

Today in our churches, God wants men and women who are on fire. Our God himself is a consuming fire **(Heb. 12:29). Samuel Pringle** gave this incredible definition of fire, "It is love; it is faith; it is hope; it is divine discontent with formality, ceremonialism, luke-warmness and indifference." It is this fire that is missing in our churches. A cold church is like cold butter—it does not spread very well.

a) Firewood Christian

If the church has to be on fire, every member of the church has to be firewood. The Holy Spirit of God would ignite the firewood to burn for His glory. How can you become firewood for Christ? First, the tree has to be cut from the earth. Your roots in the world should be cut off and plucked out of its fixtures. Then the tree is cut into pieces. You must allow the Lord to cut you and shape you according to His purpose. Sometimes He may see us through testing or through pain and suffering. These cut pieces have to be dried in the hot sun. The Lord may dry us or fry us in the sun of patience, and thus prepare us to burn for Him. These cut pieces are not immediately used in the stove or furnace. They are piled as stock in a place and used in the needed time.

The church or ministry can be compared to the stove or furnace. According to His time and purpose God takes us into His church or ministry so that we may burn for Him. This means that, we have to wait patiently in prayer and preparation in the place where God has kept us now till He leads us to a specific place and ministry. If the firewood starts burning at the stocking place, or as a tree in the forest, it will cause destruction.

b) Burning Christian

The firewood does not burn by itself. It starts burning only when the fire touches it. The Holy Spirit of God should touch us, fill us, and anoint us with His fire in order to burn for him. If the wood has not been properly dried, it will produce a lot of smoke, which would only cause tears. There are many Christians and ministers today who try to burn for Christ before even properly knowing the Lord and the Word of God, and thus they have become a hindrance to the kingdom of God and us.

When Jesus Christ becomes the best news, then we will become messengers of the good news. If you still have the witness of the world, you would only be a smoking Christian, and people would easily identify you as an immature or an unprepared witness for Christ. Hence, you must totally surrender your life to Christ and be filled with the Holy Spirit of God and allow him to be your fuel. Paul says, "...be ye filled with the Spirit" **(Eph. 5:18 KJV)**, which is a present, continuous tense, and hence, you must continue to be filled and fuelled by the Holy Spirit of God. It is easy to light a fire, but without fuel, it will not continue to burn.

c) United Christian

If the firewood burns by itself, it would very soon die out. If it burns along with two or three pieces, then it can burn well and for a longer time. Likewise, you must unite with others and minister in one spirit for an effective ministry. King Solomon said, "Two are better than one because they have a good return for their labour... And if one can overpower him who is alone, two can resist him. A chord of three strands is not quickly torn apart." **(Ecc. 4:9-12)**. From the above verses, we discover four significant benefits for those who minister together. Through mutual effort, you can have a good return for your labour **(verse 9)**. Through mutual support, you can lift up each other **(verse 10)**. Through mutual encourage-ment, you can boldly face threatening times **(verse 11)**. Through mutual strength, you can resist attacks **(verse 12)**.

d) Charcoal Christian

Good firewood will turn into charcoal after burning. It can still be used as a fuel, though not to the extent of the firewood. So, even if you become old, you can still burn in the ministry of prayer and intercession, in counseling, and writing ministry as well. The charcoal can be used till it becomes fine ash and then it flies away in thin air. Likewise, God can use you till your last breath, till you are promoted to the heavenly kingdom.

5. Fire and Mission

"The church exists by mission as fire exists by burning," said, **Emil Brunner**. The firewood does not bother about what is kept on the stove. Plain water may be heated; rice may be cooked; fish curry may be prepared; or chicken may be roasted. But the firewood keeps on burning irrespective of where and for what purpose it is utilized. Likewise, every believer from the church must be challenged and enabled to proclaim the gospel and make disciples and to be what he is called to be—in the one body of Christ, a community and a fellowship which binds people in loving interdependence, irespective of the worldly barriers of denominations, social status, race, colour, or nationality. From being a mere spectator, you must become a participant of the church ministry. Irrespective of the type of ministry and the application of it, you must totally surrender yourself to the cause of proclaiming Christ, without any conditions or reservations, like the firewood kept inside the stove. When the Lord becomes the center of our undivided attention and devotion, the success and fruit of our ministry will move from being a distant dream to an obtainable reality.

Paul says Jesus is the One Who, through His death, made it possible for diverse people to come together as spiritual brothers and sisters **(Eph. 2:11-22)**. Spiritual and relational one-ness does not always co-exist. Although people may be bound together by one Saviour, they do not automatically serve one another in love and respect through the family.

We find a prime example of unity in Joshua. An essential element of the success of the Israelites was their willingness to tackle their God-given task together. Without resistance they accepted an unusual strategy for the conquest of Jericho. By standing united in obedience to God and his chosen leader, they became an invincible force through which the Lord could carry out his work. Without jealousy, they worked as a team to accomplish God-given objectives. Without doubting, they trusted God and their leader. As a united people with a single objective, they stood as a formidable and fearsome force.

May the Lord help you to yield your life to the total control of the Holy Spirit of God to burn for Christ till the end of your life.

Chapter - 11
Faithfulness in Our Character

A scorpion, being a poor swimmer, asked a turtle to carry him on his back across a river. "Are you mad?" exclaimed the turtle. "You will sting me while I'm swimming and I'll drown."

"My dear turtle," laughed the scorpion. "If I were to sting you, you would drown and I would go down with you. Now, where is the logic in that?"

"You're right," said the turtle. "Hop on!"

The scorpion climbed aboard and halfway across the river it gave the turtle a mighty sting. As they both sank to the bottom, the turtle said, "Do you mind if I ask you something? You said there'd be no logic in you stinging me. Why then did you do it?"

"It has nothing to do with logic," the drowning scorpion sadly replied. "It's just my character."

Character is that part of a person that makes him or her different from others. Character being the crown and glory of life, lies in the will of a person. It is simply a habit long continued, but the noblest possession of man. "A man of character will make himself worthy of any position he is given" - **Mahatma Gandhi**.

It is not what we do for God that counts, but what we are before Him that matters. What we are determines the value of what we say and do. As the saying goes, "Unless there is within us that which is above, we shall soon yield to that which is around us."

Charismatic leaders have attractive personalities. Charisma is not necessarily flamboyance, loudness, or dynamism. It may be a meek and quiet spirit in the midst of a sea of boastful commercialism and slick advertising. A pocket watch and a public clock both serve the same purpose - to tell the time. If a watch goes out of order, only the owner is affected; but if a public clock goes wrong, hundreds of people are misled. So, as responsible citizens of this country, let us be examples and let not our lives be a stumbling block to others.

Peter Kusmic said, "Charisma without character is catastrophe." The circumstances amid which we live determine our reputation; the truth we believe determines our character.

1. Reputation Versus Character

Reputation is what we are supposed to be. Character is what we are.

Reputation is the photograph; character is the face. Reputation is earned in a moment;

character is built through a lifetime. Reputation is what men tell us on our tombstone; character is what angels say about us before the throne of God. Reputation is sometimes as wide as the horizon, but character is the point of a needle. A man's reputation is before men, but character is what we would do if we knew no one would ever know.

2. Character and Integrity

Integrity is what we gain by walking in God's light. "It is of far more worth than precious gold to do what's true and right." - **Dennis J.D**. Integrity is a state or quality of being complete. It is integration of a personality. In spite of severe persecution and discouragement, Job held onto his integrity. He said, "Till I die I will not put away my integrity."

A good test of a person's character is his behavior when he makes mistakes. No one goes crooked as long as he stays on the straight and narrow path. Our character is shaped by what our minds take in; we should not be like a waste paper basket. Men are more than what happens to them. Character evolves through man's beliefs, attitudes, intentions or motives and actions by which a man acquires more from history. Our reasons do not count as the real "explanation" of our behavior. You can easily judge the character of a man by how he treats those who can do nothing for him or to him.

3. Choices and Character

Choice is the starting point of action; it is the source of motion, but not the end for the sake of which we act. Little choices determine habit. Habits carve and mold character.

Why Do Even Men Of Great Reputation Fall?

Anyone can fall if his intention is to act contrary to his basic convictions or moral principles of God, and if his judgment has been clouded by "desire" or overwhelmed by "passion." Man develops character through his concrete decisions. Our decision determines our destiny. Circumstances do not make a man; they reveal what he is made of.

Theodore H. Epp said, "Lust is the bud, sin is the blossom, and death is the fruit." That is why it is important to nip temptation in the bud before it can blossom into sin and death. David was a great man, but sin defeated him. The Apostle Paul says, "Wherefore let him that thinketh he standeth take heed lest he fall" **(1 Cor. 10:12 KJV)**.

You may ask, "Can a thing like this happen to me?" Yes it can. In some unguarded moment, Satan can slip up on your weak side and set before you a temptation so alluring, that in your own strength you'll not be able to overcome it. Our trouble is not that we are tempted, but that we don't turn to God for deliverance or turn to someone for counseling when the temptation is before us.

4. Courage Sustains Character

Courage has to be sustained by the encouragement of others. Courage is the keystone in the sustenance of our character. We should have the boldness to stand for what is right, be honest and just. In times of crisis, we need the attitude of fortitude to keep us from being overcome when things run over us.

In the Bible, we find evidence of God using trials to refine Paul's character. Paul even learned to rejoice in his sufferings because he found that suffering produces endurance, and endurance produces character, and character produces hope.

Character is what we are in the dark. We can sell out character, but we cannot purchase it. The hardest trial of our character is whether we can bear a rival's failure without triumph. A man shows his character by what makes him laugh.

In the destiny of every moral being, there is an object considered more worthy by God than anything else; that is character. It exercises a greater power than wealth, and secures all honour without pining for fame. It carries with it an influence and commands the general confidence and respect of mankind.

Keeping character is easier than recovering it. Character is made by many acts; but a single one can lose it. The toughest thing in life is to remove the stains from a man's character. "Character is like a tree, and reputation is like its shadow. The shadow is what we think of it; the tree is the real thing." - **Abraham Lincoln**

The fragrance of our rich and delightful character will continue to linger about the place where we lived, as a dried rose bud scents the drawer where it has withered and perished. Purity in your heart produces power in your life. Righteousness produces beauty in your character. Do what you can, where you are, with what you have.

Printed in the United Kingdom
by Lightning Source UK Ltd.
123879UK00001BA/34-57/A